Wildcatology Trivia Challenge

Kentucky Wildcats Basketball

Wildcatology Trivia Challenge

Kentucky Wildcats Basketball

Researched by Tom P. Rippey III

Tom P. Rippey III & Paul F. Wilson, Editors

Kick The Ball, Ltd

Lewis Center, Ohio

Trivia by Kick The Ball, Ltd

College Football Trivia

Alabama Crimson Tide	Auburn Tigers	Boston College Eagles	Florida Gators
Georgia Bulldogs	LSU Tigers	Miami Hurricanes	Michigan Wolverines
Nebraska Cornhuskers	Notre Dame Fighting Irish	Ohio State Buckeyes	Oklahoma Sooners
Oregon Ducks	Penn State Nittany Lions	Southern Cal Trojans	Texas Longhorns

Pro Football Trivia

Arizona Cardinals	Buffalo Bills	Chicago Bears	Cleveland Browns
Denver Broncos	Green Bay Packers	Indianapolis Colts	Kansas City Chiefs
Minnesota Vikings	New England Patriots	New Orleans Saints	New York Giants
New York Jets	Oakland Raiders	Philadelphia Eagles	Pittsburgh Steelers
San Francisco 49ers	Washington Redskins		

Pro Baseball Trivia

Boston Red Sox	Chicago Cubs	Chicago White Sox	Cincinnati Reds
Detroit Tigers	Los Angeles Dodgers	New York Mets	New York Yankees
Philadelphia Phillies	Saint Louis Cardinals	San Francisco Giants	

College Basketball Trivia

Duke Blue Devils	Georgetown Hoyas	Indiana Hoosiers	Kansas Jayhawks
Kentucky Wildcats	Maryland Terrapins	Michigan State Spartans	North Carolina Tar Heels
Syracuse Orange	UConn Huskies	UCLA Bruins	

Pro Basketball Trivia

Boston Celtics	Chicago Bulls	Detroit Pistons	Los Angeles Lakers
Utah Jazz			

Visit **www.TriviaGameBooks.com** for more details.

This book is dedicated to our families and friends for your unwavering love, support, and your understanding of our pursuit of our passions. Thank you for everything you do for us and for making our lives complete.

**Wildcatology Trivia Challenge: Kentucky Wildcats Basketball;
Fourth Edition 2010**

Published by
Kick The Ball, Ltd
8595 Columbus Pike, Suite 197
Lewis Center, OH 43035
www.TriviaGameBooks.com

Designed, Formatted, and Edited by: Tom P. Rippey III & Paul F. Wilson
Researched by: Tom P. Rippey III

For information on ordering this book in bulk at reduced prices, please email us at pfwilson@triviagamebooks.com.

International Standard Book Number: 978-1-934372-92-0

Printed and Bound in the United States of America

10 9 8 7 6 5 4 3 2 1

Table of Contents

Dear Friend,

Thank you for purchasing our *Wildcatology Trivia Challenge* game book!

We have made every attempt to verify the accuracy of the questions and answers contained in this book. However it is still possible that from time to time an error has been made by us or our researchers. In the event you find a question or answer that is questionable or inaccurate, we ask for your understanding and thank you for bringing it to our attention so we may improve future editions of this book. Please email us at tprippey@triviagamebooks.com with those observations and comments.

Have fun playing *Wildcatology Trivia Challenge*!

Tom & Paul

Tom Rippey & Paul Wilson
Co-Founders, Kick The Ball, Ltd

PS – You can discover more about all of our current trivia game books by visiting www.TriviaGameBooks.com.

Book Format:

There are four quarters, each made up of fifty questions. Each quarter's questions have assigned point values. Questions are designed to get progressively more difficult as you proceed through each quarter, as well as through the book itself. Most questions are in a four-option multiple-choice format so that you will at least have a 25% chance of getting a correct answer for some of the more challenging questions.

We have even added an overtime section in the event of a tie, or just in case you want to keep playing a little longer.

Game Options:

One Player -
To play on your own, simply answer each of the questions in all the quarters, and in the overtime section, if you'd like. Use the Player / Team Score Sheet to record your answers and the quarter Answer Keys to check your answers. Calculate each quarter's points and the total for the game at the bottom of the Player / Team Score Sheet to determine your final score.

Two or More Players –
To play with multiple players decide if you will all be competing with each other individually, or if you will form and play as teams. Each player / team will then have its own Player / Team Score Sheet to record its answer. You can use the quarter Answer Keys to check your answers and to calculate your final scores.

The Player / Team Score Sheets have been designed so that each team can answer all questions or you can divide the questions up in any combination you would prefer. For example, you may want to alternate questions if two players are playing or answer every third question for three players, etc. In any case, simply record your response to your questions in the corresponding quarter and question number on the Player / Team Score Sheet.

A winner will be determined by multiplying the total number of correct answers for each quarter by the point value per quarter, then adding together the final total for all quarters combined. Play the game again and again by alternating the questions that your team is assigned so that you will answer a different set of questions each time you play.

You Create the Game -
There are countless other ways of using *Wildcatology Trivia Challenge* questions. It is limited only to your imagination. Examples might be using them at your tailgate or other college basketball related party. Players / Teams who answer questions incorrectly may have to perform a required action, or winners may receive special prizes. Let us know what other games you come up with!

Have fun!

1) What year did the nickname Wildcats become widely associated with the University of Kentucky?

Answers begin on page 17

   A) 1901
   B) 1909
   C) 1915
   D) 1923

2) What are the Wildcats' official colors?

   A) Navy Blue and Cream
   B) Blue and White
   C) Black and Gold
   D) Blue and Cream

3) What is the name of Kentucky's current home arena?

   A) Wildcat Field House
   B) Pitino Arena
   C) Derby Field House
   D) Rupp Arena

4) How many Naismith College Player of the Year winners played at Kentucky?

   A) 0
   B) 2
   C) 4
   D) 5

5) What is the name of Kentucky's fight song?

    A) "My Old Kentucky Home"
    B) "Kentucky Fight"
    C) "On, On, U of K"
    D) "UK Alma Mater"

6) How many UK players have won an Olympic gold medal for basketball?

    A) 3
    B) 5
    C) 9
    D) 12

7) How many times has Kentucky appeared in the NCAA Final Four?

    A) 7
    B) 9
    C) 11
    D) 13

8) Who had the longest coaching tenure at Kentucky?

    A) Adolph Rupp
    B) Rick Pitino
    C) Tubby Smith
    D) Eddie Sutton

9) What year did Kentucky join the SEC?

    A) 1926
    B) 1929
    C) 1932
    D) 1937

10) Which SEC opponent has Kentucky played the most in the regular season?

    A) Vanderbilt
    B) Georgia
    C) Alabama
    D) Tennessee

11) Who led the Wildcats in total rebounds in the 2009-10 season?

    A) Daniel Orton
    B) DeMarcus Cousins
    C) John Wall
    D) Patrick Patterson

12) The seating capacity of Rupp Arena is greater than 20,000.

    A) True
    B) False

13) What is the name of Kentucky's costumed mascot?

A) Wally
B) Wildcat
C) Wilson
D) Woodrow

14) Which famous Wildcat radio play-by-play broadcaster has a jersey retired in his memory?

A) Jim Williams
B) Hank "Talk 'em Blue" Jacobs
C) Cawood Ledford
D) Tom Jones

15) What year was Kentucky's first-ever overtime game?

A) 1907
B) 1911
C) 1918
D) 1921

16) What year did the Wildcats play their first-ever game?

A) 1898
B) 1903
C) 1905
D) 1907

17) Did Kentucky score over 2,500 points as a team in the 2009-10 season?

    A) Yes
    B) No

18) What arena is Kentucky's "home away from home"?

    A) McBrayer Arena
    B) Racer Arena
    C) E.A. Diddle Arena
    D) Freedom Hall

19) What was the University of Kentucky originally known as?

    A) Always known as the University of Kentucky
    B) Kentucky Tech
    C) Lexington University
    D) Kentucky State College

20) Who was the first-ever consensus All-American at Kentucky?

    A) Ralph Beard
    B) Gayle Rose
    C) Basil Hayden
    D) Alex Groza

21) Did Kentucky have a winning record its first-ever season?

    A) Yes
    B) No

22) What nickname was given to the 1948 KU basketball team?

    A) Fantastic Five
    B) Sweet Team
    C) Fabulous Five
    D) Racing Rockets

23) Which Kentucky coach has the most all-time career wins?

    A) Tubby Smith
    B) Rick Pitino
    C) Joe Hall
    D) Adolph Rupp

24) Which of the following Wildcats was only chosen once to the All-NCAA Final Four Team?

    A) Pat Riley
    B) Ron Mercer
    C) Alex Groza
    D) Scott Padgett

25) Who holds UK's record for assists in a single game?

A) Travis Ford
B) Anthony Epps
C) Sean Woods
D) John Wall

26) When was UK's first-ever undefeated season?

A) 1905-06
B) 1911-12
C) 1920-21
D) 1928-29

27) What is UK's record for most consecutive NCAA Tournament appearances?

A) 13
B) 15
C) 19
D) 21

28) Who was Kentucky's first-ever official basketball coach?

A) Alpha Brumage
B) J.J. Tigert
C) S.A. Boles
D) E.R. Sweetland

29) The Wildcats had only one undefeated season under Coach Rupp.

   A) True
   B) False

30) Excluding Louisville, which opponent did UK last face in Freedom Hall?

   A) UAB
   B) Indiana
   C) Houston
   D) Appalachian State

31) What was UK's home arena prior to Rupp Arena?

   A) Augustus Gymnasium
   B) Memorial Coliseum
   C) Big Blue Arena
   D) Alumni Field House

32) How many overtime games did UK play in the 2009-10 season?

   A) 1
   B) 3
   C) 4
   D) 6

33) What is the total number of seasons the Wildcats have gone undefeated at home?

    A) 19
    B) 21
    C) 28
    D) 30

34) How many times has Kentucky's men's basketball team been named the CATSPY Team of the Year?

    A) 0
    B) 3
    C) 5
    D) 8

35) Who was the only opponent to score greater than 90 points against Kentucky in the 2009-10 season?

    A) Sam Houston
    B) Florida
    C) Louisville
    D) West Virginia

36) How many times has Kentucky led the nation in three-pointers made in a season?

    A) 0
    B) 1
    C) 3
    D) 5

37) Which opposing player holds the record for most points scored in a single game against Kentucky?

A) Bill Russell
B) Magic Johnson
C) Larry Bird
D) Pete Maravich

38) Kentucky has more SEC Tournament titles than all other current SEC teams combined.

A) True
B) False

39) What is the nickname of the student section at Rupp Arena?

A) Wiley Wildcats
B) eRUPPtion Zone
C) Pride Zone
D) Claws

40) What did Rick Pitino call his full-court press at Kentucky?

A) Lemon squeeze press
B) Steamroller
C) Mother-in-law press
D) Hard court press

41) How many NCAA National Championships has Kentucky won?

    A) 5
    B) 7
    C) 9
    D) 10

42) Since 1903, what is the only season Kentucky did not play basketball?

    A) 1952-53
    B) 1956-57
    C) 1962-63
    D) 1971-72

43) Who was the Wildcats' first-ever opponent at Rupp Arena?

    A) Louisville
    B) Dartmouth
    C) Wisconsin
    D) DePaul

44) In the 2009-10 season, which team handed Kentucky its first loss?

    A) Florida
    B) Tennessee
    C) Alabama
    D) South Carolina

45) Who holds UK's record for career blocks?

    A) Sam Bowie
    B) Chuck Hayes
    C) Andre Riddick
    D) Jamaal Magloire

46) Which season did Kentucky have two First Team Consensus All-Americans?

    A) 1946-47
    B) 1965-66
    C) 1977-78
    D) 1983-84

47) What are the most losses in one season by Kentucky at Rupp Arena?

    A) 6
    B) 8
    C) 9
    D) 11

48) Who holds Kentucky's record for points scored in a single game?

    A) Tayshaun Prince
    B) Dan Issel
    C) Jodie Meeks
    D) Louie Dampier

49) Does Kentucky have an all-time winning record in overtime games?

    A) Yes
    B) No

50) What year did Kentucky first celebrate a victory over Louisville?

    A) 1910
    B) 1913
    C) 1925
    D) 1928

In 1977, top ranked Kentucky had one trying night. They were playing at Allen Field House in Adolph Rupp's home state of Kansas, in a game dedicated "Adolph Rupp Night." In an ironic and tragic twist, Rupp would die at age 76 that very night at a University of Kentucky Medical Center in Lexington, Ky. On the court, the Wildcats battled the Jayhawks, eventually winning the game in a final score of 73-66. Although the game was won, Wildcat Nation and the world of basketball lost one of the sport's true icons. Perhaps inspired by the legacy and memory of the "Baron of the Bluegrass" the Wildcats went on to win the National Championship that season.

1) B – 1909 (The head of the military department said the football team "fought like wildcats" following a road victory against Illinois.)

2) B – Blue and White (These colors were officially adopted by the University in 1892.)

3) D – Rupp Arena (The arena opened in 1976, having a construction cost of $53 million.)

4) A – 0 (The Naismith Award was first awarded in 1969 and to date no UK players have won the award.)

5) C – "On, On, U of K" (The song was written by Carl A. Lambert in the 1920s.)

6) C – 9 (Wallace Jones [1948], Cliff Barker [1948], Ralph Beard [1948], Alex Groza [1948], Kenny Rollins [1948], Billy Evans [1956], Adrian Smith [1960], Sam Bowie [1980], and Tayshaun Prince [2008])

7) D – 13 (1942, 1948, 1949, 1951, 1958, 1966, 1975, 1978, 1984, 1993, 1996, 1997, and 1998)

8) A – Adolph Rupp (He coached the Wildcats for 42 years from 1931-72.)

9) C – 1932 (The SEC was formed in 1932. Kentucky is one of the conference's thirteen founding members.)

10) D – Tennessee (The Wildcats have played the Volunteers a total of 209 times and hold a 143-66 series advantage, for a .684 winning percentage.)

11) B – DeMarcus Cousins (He finished the season with 376 total rebounds [156 offensive and 220 defensive].)

12) A – True (The official seating capacity of Rupp Arena is 23,000.)

13) B – Wildcat (He first appeared at games in 1976. The more kid-friendly mascot, Scratch, appeared in the 1990s. Both mascots still attend football and basketball games today.)

14) C – Cawood Ledford (He was the "Voice of the Wildcats" from 1953-92. Ledford was inducted into the Naismith Memorial Basketball Hall of Fame in 1994. He died in 2001.)

15) A – 1907 (Kentucky lost 23-25 to Central University.)

16) B – 1903 (Kentucky fell 6-15 to Georgetown [KY] on Feb. 6, 1903.)

17) A – Yes (UK scored a total of 3,012 points while holding opponents to a combined 2,,468 points.)

18) D – Freedom Hall (Located in Louisville, the Wildcats first played at Freedom Hall in 1958. UK has a 56-17 all-time record at the arena, for a .767 winning percentage.)

19) D – Kentucky State College (The school went by this name until 1908.)

20) C – Basil Hayden (He became UK's first-ever consensus All-American in 1921.)

21) B – No (The Wildcats went 1-2 their first-ever season. UK's only win came against Lexington YMCA [UK 11, YMCA 10].)

22) C – Fabulous Five (This nickname was given by Adolph Rupp. The team was Kentucky's first-ever National Championship team.)

23) D – Adolph Rupp (He coached the Wildcats to 876 wins from 1931-72.)

24) A – Pat Riley (His only selection to the All-NCAA Final Four Team was in 1966.)

25) D – John Wall (He had 16 assists versus Hartford on Dec. 29, 2009.)

26) B – 1911-12 (The Wildcats finished 9-0.)

27) C – 19 (UK appeared in the NCAA Tournament every year from 1992-2010.)

28) D – E.R. Sweetland (He signed a three-year deal in 1910 making him Kentucky's coach and athletic director.)

29) A – True (Rupp's only undefeated season was the 1953-54 season when his Wildcats went 25-0. The only other coach to record an undefeated season at Kentucky was E.R. Sweetland. He led UK to a 9-0 record in the 1911-12 season.)

30) D – Appalachian State (The Wildcats beat the Mountaineers 93-69 on Dec. 20, 2008.)

31) B – Memorial Coliseum (The Wildcats played here from 1950-76. Seating capacity was 11,500.)

32) B – 3 (Kentucky went into overtime once with Stanford and twice with Mississippi State. The Wildcats won all three games.)

33) C – 28 (Most recently in the 2009-10 season. UK also has 28 seasons with only one home loss for a total of 56 seasons with no more than one home loss.)

34) B – 3 (The CATSPY Awards began in 2003 to honor athletes in all sports at the University of Kentucky. The men's basketball team was honored as Men's Team of the Year in 2003, 2005, and 2010.)

35) A – Sam Houston (The Wildcats beat the Bearkats 102-92 on Nov. 19, 2009.)

36) C – 3 (1992 [317 three-pointers], 1993 [340 three-pointers], and 1994 [301 three-pointers])

37) D – Pete Maravich (He scored 64 points against
Kentucky in 1970.)

38) A – True (UK has 26 SEC Tournament titles compared
to a combined 24 titles for the rest of the SEC.)

39) B – eRUPPtion Zone (The eRUPPtion zone helps make
Rupp Arena arguably one of the most intimidating
places to play in college basketball.)

40) C – Mother-in-law press (Pitino chose this name
because of the non-stop pressure and harassment.)

41) B – 7 (1948, 1949, 1951, 1958, 1978, 1996, and 1998)

42) A – 1952-53 (The Wildcats were banned from play due
to NCAA sanctions.)

43) C – Wisconsin (UK beat the Badgers 72-64 in the first-
ever game at Rupp Arena.)

44) D – South Carolina (The Wildcats lost 62-68 to the
Gamecocks on Jan. 26, 2010.)

45) D – Jamaal Magloire (He recorded 268 blocks from
1997-2000.)

46) A – 1946-47 (Ralph Beard [Guard] and Alex Groza
[Center])

47) A – 6 (In the 1988-89 season, the Wildcats finished 8-6
at home.)

48) C – Jodie Meeks (Meeks scored 54 points against Tennessee on Jan. 13, 2009. The record was previously held for 30 years by Dan Issel when he scored 53 against Ole Miss in 1970.)

49) A – Yes (The Wildcats are 51-42 all-time in overtime games, for a .548 winning percentage.)

50) B – 1913 (UK beat Louisville 34-10 in the first-ever meeting between the schools.)

Note: All answers valid as of the end of the 2009-10 season, unless otherwise indicated in the question itself.

1) How many times has Kentucky won by 60 or more points?

Answers begin on page 37

   A) 9
   B) 12
   C) 14
   D) 15

2) Which Kentucky player led the team in assists in the 2009-10 season?

   A) Ramon Harris
   B) Eric Bledsoe
   C) John Wall
   D) Darius Miller

3) Which coach had the second longest tenure at Kentucky?

   A) Tubby Smith
   B) Rick Pitino
   C) Joe Hall
   D) George Buchheit

4) How many decades has Kentucky won at least 225 games?

   A) 2
   B) 4
   C) 6
   D) 7

5) What was the name of the first athletic conference to which Kentucky belonged?

- A) Southern Intercollegiate Athletic Association
- B) Ohio Valley Conference
- C) Southern Conference
- D) Atlantic Athletic Conference

6) Has Kentucky ever played 40 or more games in a single season?

- A) Yes
- B) No

7) Which opposing player holds the record for most rebounds against Kentucky in a single game?

- A) Shaquille O'Neal
- B) Christian Laettner
- C) Marcus Camby
- D) Rick Kelley

8) What is UK's record for largest margin of victory over an opponent?

- A) 51 points
- B) 59 points
- C) 68 points
- D) 77 points

9) How many times has Kentucky beaten a team ranked No. 1 in the AP Poll?

    A) 3
    B) 5
    C) 6
    D) 8

10) Has Kentucky ever lost to any of the U.S. Service Academies?

    A) Yes
    B) No

11) What is Kentucky's all-time winning percentage against Louisville?

    A) .541
    B) .583
    C) .630
    D) .659

12) Which non-conference opponent has Kentucky played the most?

    A) Louisville
    B) Cincinnati
    C) Indiana
    D) Georgia Tech

13) How many times has Kentucky played in a game that went into triple overtime?

    A) 4
    B) 6
    C) 8
    D) 11

14) Who holds Kentucky's career record for points scored?

    A) Pat Riley
    B) Dan Issel
    C) Jamal Mashburn
    D) Rex Chapman

15) What is UK's record for the most fouls committed as a team in a single game?

    A) 28
    B) 31
    C) 35
    D) 39

16) Which team handed Kentucky its worst-ever loss?

    A) Tennessee
    B) Vanderbilt
    C) Boston College
    D) Central University

17) To how many consecutive NCAA Tournaments did Rick Pitino coach Kentucky?

   A) 4
   B) 5
   C) 6
   D) 8

18) In the 2009-10 season, what were the fewest points Kentucky allowed in a single game?

   A) 35
   B) 39
   C) 41
   D) 44

19) What is UK's longest winning streak in the Kentucky-Louisville series?

   A) 3
   B) 5
   C) 7
   D) 9

20) Have the Wildcats won 100 or more NCAA Tournament games?

   A) Yes
   B) No

21) Who is the only Kentucky player to be named SEC Men's Basketball Player of the Year more than once?

  A) Kenny Walker
  B) Pat Riley
  C) Ron Mercer
  D) Tom Parker

22) How many all-time AP Top-10 finishes does Kentucky have?

  A) 28
  B) 31
  C) 35
  D) 39

23) Which of the following Wildcats was not named Consensus First Team All-American, SEC Player of the Year, and to the All-NCAA Final Four Team?

  A) Ron Mercer
  B) Tony Delk
  C) Pat Riley
  D) Jamal Mashburn

24) All-time, what are the fewest points a Kentucky team has allowed in a single game?

  A) 0
  B) 6
  C) 10
  D) 18

25) Which UK head coach has the second most all-time career wins?

  A) Rick Pitino
  B) George Buchheit
  C) Joe Hall
  D) Eddie Sutton

26) Did the Wildcats have a game in the 2009-10 season in which they scored fewer than 50 points?

  A) Yes
  B) No

27) What is the largest second-half deficit a Wildcats team has overcome in victory?

  A) 19 points
  B) 23 points
  C) 26 points
  D) 31 points

28) What is Kentucky's individual record for most rebounds in a single game?

  A) 16
  B) 20
  C) 25
  D) 34

29) All-time, how many of Kentucky's games have gone into overtime?

A) 5
B) 7
C) 9
D) 11

30) What is UK's record for consecutive winning seasons?

A) 35
B) 43
C) 52
D) 60

31) Who was Kentucky's first-ever NCAA Tournament opponent?

A) Illinois
B) Wake Forest
C) Texas
D) Villanova

32) How many times have Kentucky players won SEC Player of the Year?

A) 6
B) 8
C) 12
D) 14

33) What is Kentucky's team record for most three-pointers made in a single game?

A) 18
B) 19
C) 21
D) 25

34) How many times has Kentucky played in the Postseason NIT Tournament?

A) 5
B) 8
C) 10
D) 13

35) How many points was UK's largest loss to Louisville?

A) 22
B) 25
C) 28
D) 31

36) How many times has Kentucky finished No. 1 in the final AP Poll?

A) 6
B) 8
C) 10
D) 12

37) Who led the Wildcats in free-throw percentage in the 2009-10 season (minimum 25 attempts)?

A) Patrick Patterson
B) Darnell Dodson
C) John Wall
D) Darius Miller

38) How many times have Kentucky players been named to the All-NCAA Final Four Team?

A) 16
B) 18
C) 20
D) 23

39) Who holds Kentucky's record for steals in a season?

A) Rajon Rondo
B) Wayne Turner
C) Derek Anderson
D) Rex Chapman

40) Which season did the Wildcats first record 20 wins?

A) 1921-22
B) 1925-26
C) 1932-33
D) 1939-40

41) Against which conference opponent does Kentucky have the most all-time wins in the regular season?

A) Vanderbilt
B) Georgia
C) Mississippi State
D) Tennessee

42) Which team did the Wildcats play in their first game of the 2010 NCAA Tournament?

A) Wake Forest
B) Cornell
C) East Tennessee State
D) West Virginia

43) Who holds Kentucky's record for most games played in a career?

A) Wayne Turner
B) Jamal Mashburn
C) Sam Bowie
D) Jamaal Magloire

44) What is UK's record for most consecutive SEC regular-season titles?

A) 6
B) 7
C) 9
D) 11

45) Has a Kentucky player ever led the nation in scoring?

    A) Yes
    B) No

46) What is Kentucky's all-time consecutive home wins record?

    A) 111
    B) 119
    C) 129
    D) 136

47) In the 2009-10 season, how many Kentucky players averaged 10 or more points per game?

    A) 2
    B) 4
    C) 6
    D) 8

48) Which non-conference opponent has the most wins against Kentucky?

    A) Notre Dame
    B) Duke
    C) Indiana
    D) Georgia Tech

49) What season did Kentucky win its first regular season SEC title?

   A) 1932-33
   B) 1935-36
   C) 1939-40
   D) 1942-43

50) Who was Kentucky's opponent both times they appeared in the Jimmy V Classic?

   A) Syracuse
   B) Duke
   C) Kansas
   D) Michigan

Regular Season / Cool Fact
Wildcatology Trivia Challenge

In the 1951 NCAA Championship game, the Wildcats had only six healthy players available to play. Kansas State jumped out to a 20-12 lead and it looked like Kentucky was done for. Coach Rupp inserted freshman Cliff Hagan, who was suffering from an infected throat. Hagan sparked a rally that led the Wildcats to within two points at halftime. Hagan and Bill Spivey then led a second-half charge as Kentucky outscored Kansas State 41-29 to win its third National Championship.

1) B – 12 (The last time Kentucky won by 60 or more points was against Vanderbilt in the 2002-03 season [UK 106, Vandy 44].)

2) C – John Wall (He led the team with 241 assists.)

3) C – Joe Hall (He coached the Wildcats for 13 seasons from 1973-85.)

4) B – 4 (2000s [275 wins], 1990s [291 wins], 1970s [276 wins], and 1940s [249 wins])

5) A – Southern Intercollegiate Athletic Association (The first athletic conference formed in the United States in 1895, of which Kentucky was a founding member. The conference split in 1921 to form the Southern Conference which later became the SEC.)

6) A – Yes (The Wildcats played a total of 40 games in the 1996-97 season, finishing with a 35-5 record.)

7) D – Rick Kelley (He recorded 27 rebounds for Stanford in 1974 [UK 78, Stanford 77].)

8) D – 77 points (In 1956, Kentucky beat Georgia 143-66.)

9) C – 6 (The last time the Wildcats beat a team ranked No. 1 in the AP Poll was Florida in 2003 [UK 70, Florida 55].)

10) A – Yes (Kentucky leads the series with Air Force [1-0], Army [1-0], and Navy [4-1].)

11) D – .659 (Kentucky leads the series 27-14.)

12) D – Georgia Tech (The Wildcats have played the Yellow Jackets a total of 71 times and hold a 56-15 series advantage, for a .789 winning percentage. Georgia Tech was a member of the SEC until 1964.)

13) A – 4 (The Wildcats are undefeated in triple-overtime games beating Centre College 22-20 in 1918, Miami (Ohio) 43-42 in 1928, Temple 85-83 in 1957, and Vanderbilt 79-73 in 2008.)

14) B – Dan Issel (He scored a career 2,138 points in 83 games from 1968-70.)

15) C – 35 (This record was set against Auburn in 1981.)

16) D – Central University (Kentucky lost 17-87 to Central University in 1910.)

17) C – 6 (Pitino led the Wildcats to the NCAA Tournament from 1992-97, his last six seasons with UK.)

18) D – 44 (Kentucky beat Drexel 88-44.)

19) B – 5 (UK beat Louisville five straight meetings from 1916-51.)

20) A – Yes (The Wildcats have an all-time NCAA Tournament record of 101-45, for a .692 winning percentage.)

21) A – Kenny Walker (1985 and 1986)

22) D – 39 (The last time the Wildcats finished in the top 10 was a No. 2-ranking following the 2009-10 season.)

23) C – Pat Riley (He was named SEC Player of the Year, and to the All-NCAA Final Four Team, but was only Second Team All-American.)

24) B – 6 (In 1945, Kentucky held Arkansas State to six points.)

25) C – Joe Hall (He coached the Wildcats to 297 wins from 1973-85.)

26) B – No (The lowest point total for UK in 2009-10 was 62 points against South Carolina and Cornell.)

27) D – 31 points (In the 1993-94 season, UK was losing 37-68 to LSU with 15:34 left in the game. Kentucky came back to win 99-95.)

28) D – 34 (This record is held by both Bob Burrow [1955] and Bill Spivey [1951].)

29) C – 9 (Kentucky holds a 4-5 record in NCAA overtime games, for a .444 winning percentage.)

30) D – 60 (UK had a winning record every season from 1927-28 through 1987-88 [they did not play the 1952-53 season].)

31) A – Illinois (The Wildcats played the Fighting Illini in the 1942 NCAA Tournament [UK 46, Illinois 44].)

32) C – 12 (Pat Riley [1966], Tom Parker [1972], Kevin Grevey [1973], Kyle Macy [1980], Kenny Walker [1985 and 1986], Jamal Mashburn [1993], Tony Delk [1996], Ron Mercer [1997], Tayshaun Prince [2001], Keith Bogans [2003], and John Wall [2010])

33) C – 21 (UK made 21 of 48 three-pointers against North Carolina in 1989 [UK 110, UNC 121].)

34) B – 8 (1944, 1946, 1947, 1949, 1950, 1976, 1979 and 2009 [UK won the tournament in 1946 and 1976.])

35) A – 22 (In 1988, the Wildcats fell 75-97 to the Cardinals.)

36) B – 8 (1949, 1951, 1952, 1954, 1966, 1970, 1978, and 2003)

37) D – Darius Miller (He made 31 of 39 attempts, for a .795 free-throw percentage.)

38) B – 18 (Alex Groza [1948 and 1949], Shelby Linville [1951], Bill Spivey [1951], Vernon Hatton [1958], Johnny Cox [1958], Louie Dampier [1966], Pat Riley [1966], Kevin Grevey [1975], Jack Givens [1978], Rick Robey [1978], Jamal Mashburn [1993], Tony Delk [1996], Ron Mercer [1996 and 1997], Scott Padgett [1997 and 1998], and Jeff Sheppard [1998])

39) A – Rajon Rondo (He had 87 steals in the 2004-05 season.)

40) C – 1932-33 (Kentucky finished the season 21-3.)

41) D – Tennessee (The Wildcats have beaten the Volunteers 143 times.)

42) C – East Tennessee State (The Wildcats beat the Buccaneers 100-71 in the first round of the tournament.)

43) A – Wayne Turner (He played a total of 151 games from 1996-99.)

44) C – 9 (The Wildcats won the regular-season SEC title from 1943-44 through 1951-52.)

45) B – No (Dan Issel came the closest in 1970 when he was the nation's fourth leading scorer with an average of 33.9 points per game.)

46) C – 129 (UK won every home game from Jan. 4, 1943 to Jan. 8, 1955.)

47) B – 4 (John Wall [16.6], DeMarcus Cousins [15.1], Patrick Patterson [14.3], and Eric Bledsoe [11.3])

48) C – Indiana (UK has lost a total of 23 times to the Hoosiers. All-time, Kentucky leads the series 30-23, for a .566 winning percentage.)

49) A – 1932-33 (UK was 21-3 that season, winning the inaugural season of the SEC.)

50) B – Duke (The Wildcats played in the Jimmy V Classic in 1998 [UK 60, Duke 71] and 2001 [UK 92, Duke 95].)

Note: All answers valid as of the end of the 2009-10 season, unless otherwise indicated in the question itself.

Wildcatology Trivia Challenge

1) How many times has Kentucky appeared in the SEC Tournament Championship game?

Answers begin on page 56

    A) 28
    B) 31
    C) 35
    D) 37

2) Who holds UK's record for free throws made in a single game?

    A) Dwight Anderson
    B) Johnny Cox
    C) Fred Cowan
    D) Rodrick Rhodes

3) Which season did the Wildcats first record 30 wins?

    A) 1935-36
    B) 1939-40
    C) 1942-43
    D) 1946-47

4) Did any Wildcat have 50 or more steals in the 2009-10 season?

    A) Yes
    B) No

5) What are the most consecutive games the Wildcats have won at Madison Square Garden?

A) 5
B) 7
C) 9
D) 11

6) What is UK's record for most consecutive winning seasons?

A) 29
B) 32
C) 38
D) 41

7) What name did the University of Kentucky go by from 1908 to 1916?

A) Kentucky University
B) University of Lexington
C) Kentucky State University
D) Kentucky College of Science and Industry

8) In the UK Alma Mater, what does the color blue represent?

A) Sky
B) Sea
C) Happiness
D) Future

9) What is UK's record for consecutive home-opening wins?

A) 28
B) 34
C) 36
D) 39

10) Which decade were the most Wildcats named First Team Consensus All-American?

A) 1940s
B) 1950s
C) 1970s
D) 1990s

11) Who holds Kentucky's record for steals in a career?

A) Wayne Turner
B) Chuck Hayes
C) Dirk Minniefield
D) Keith Bogans

12) Who holds KU's single-game freshman scoring record?

A) John Wall
B) Rex Chapman
C) Sam Bowie
D) Jamal Mashburn

13) Who coached the Wildcats immediately prior to Adolph Rupp?

    A)   John Mauer
    B)   Basil Hayden
    C)   Ray Eklund
    D)   Andrew Gill

14) Has Kentucky ever had a player drafted No. 1 overall in the NBA Draft?

    A)   Yes
    B)   No

15) What is KU's largest margin of victory against Louisville?

    A)   28 points
    B)   31 points
    C)   34 points
    D)   40 points

16) How many players on the 2009-10 KU roster were from the state of Kentucky?

    A)   1
    B)   3
    C)   4
    D)   6

17) Does Adolph Rupp have the highest winning percentage of any college basketball coach with at least 500 wins?

   A) Yes
   B) No

18) Which team snapped the UK record for consecutive home-opening wins?

   A) Clemson
   B) Tulsa
   C) Ohio State
   D) Virginia Tech

19) In the UK Alma Mater, what does the color white represent?

   A) Lofty clouds
   B) Courage
   C) Pride
   D) Stainless page

20) Who ran Kentucky's teams their first seven seasons, from 1903 through 1909?

   A) Athletic Directors
   B) Coaches
   C) Managers
   D) Players

21) Against which team was the last regular-season SEC loss for the Wildcats in 2009-10 season?

   A) Florida
   B) Georgia
   C) Tennessee
   D) Vanderbilt

22) Was Jamal Mashburn ever a team captain at Kentucky?

   A) Yes
   B) No

23) How many all-time appearances has UK made in the NCAA Tournament?

   A) 39
   B) 43
   C) 51
   D) 56

24) Since 1938, what is UK's record for fewest points scored in a game?

   A) 24
   B) 29
   C) 32
   D) 37

25) What year was the first-ever televised UK basketball game?

    A) 1948
    B) 1951
    C) 1955
    D) 1958

26) How many times has Kentucky appeared in the NCAA Tournament Championship game?

    A) 7
    B) 9
    C) 10
    D) 12

27) What is UK's record for most consecutive SEC Tournament Championships?

    A) 5
    B) 7
    C) 8
    D) 10

28) Who was the first-ever black player to sign with Kentucky?

    A) Tom Payne
    B) Jack Givens
    C) Sam Bowie
    D) Sean Woods

29) What is UK's record for most consecutive SEC losses?

A) 3
B) 5
C) 6
D) 9

30) Did Kentucky win greater than 90 percent of their games while playing at Alumni Gym?

A) Yes
B) No

31) Who scored Kentucky's first points in the 2010 NCAA Tournament?

A) DeMarcus Cousins
B) Patrick Patterson
C) John Wall
D) Darius Miller

32) What is UK's record for most points scored in one half?

A) 69
B) 74
C) 79
D) 86

33) How many times has Kentucky been beaten while ranked No. 1 in the AP Poll?

    A) 15
    B) 19
    C) 23
    D) 26

34) In which category did UK not lead the nation in 1997?

    A) Three-pointers made
    B) Total points
    C) Assists
    D) Steals

35) What are the most consecutive SEC Tournament Championship games Kentucky has lost?

    A) 2
    B) 3
    C) 4
    D) 6

36) How many Kentucky head coaches lasted one season or less?

    A) 4
    B) 6
    C) 8
    D) 9

Wildcatology Trivia Challenge

37) Which season did UK lead the nation in blocked shots?

    A) 1961-62
    B) 1982-83
    C) 1997-98
    D) 2001-02

38) Which team gave UK its first-ever home loss at Rupp Arena?

    A) Tennessee
    B) Mississippi State
    C) Tulane
    D) Washington

39) Which SEC school has the highest winning percentage against the Wildcats?

    A) Vanderbilt
    B) LSU
    C) Florida
    D) Tennessee

40) What is Kentucky's record for most losses in one season at Memorial Coliseum?

    A) 5
    B) 7
    C) 8
    D) 10

41) What is UK's record for most consecutive NCAA Tournament wins?

    A) 7
    B) 10
    C) 12
    D) 14

42) Who was the first-ever Wildcat to appear on the cover of *Sports Illustrated*?

    A) Ralph Beard
    B) Alex Groza
    C) Pat Riley
    D) Sam Bowie

43) Which coach started the famous season-opening Midnight Practice at Kentucky?

    A) Adolph Rupp
    B) Tubby Smith
    C) Rick Pitino
    D) Joe Hall

44) Who is the only Wildcat to win a High School State, NCAA, and NBA Championship?

    A) Derek Anderson
    B) Rick Robey
    C) Jamal Mashburn
    D) Dan Issel

45) In what year did Kentucky win, what is believed to be, the first-ever college basketball tournament?

  A) 1913
  B) 1917
  C) 1921
  D) 1925

46) How much money was raised by the players in 1903 to form the Kentucky basketball team?

  A) $3.00
  B) $4.10
  C) $5.45
  D) $6.70

47) When was the most recent season Kentucky led the nation in scoring margin?

  A) 1977-78
  B) 1989-90
  C) 1992-93
  D) 1996-97

48) How many Wildcats are in the Naismith Memorial Basketball Hall of Fame as players?

  A) 2
  B) 4
  C) 7
  D) 9

49) In the 2009-10 regular season, how many times did the Wildcats win a game when trailing at halftime?

    A) 1
    B) 2
    C) 4
    D) 5

50) What is Kentucky's record for most consecutive SEC wins?

    A) 46
    B) 49
    C) 51
    D) 59

One reason the plans for Memorial Coliseum were approved by the heads of the University of Kentucky was to provide a larger home to seat the growing number of Wildcat fans. After winning 12 SEC Tournament Championships and two National Titles, the 2,800 seats at Alumni Gym began to provide "riot" like atmospheres not only for opponents, but also for fellow UK fans. Fights were common. Those lucky enough to get inside would commonly have to fight for a seat to cheer on their beloved Wildcats. Eventually Wildcat Nation outgrew the 11,500 seat Memorial Coliseum, which led to the approval to construct Rupp Arena.

1) C – 35 (Their first appearance was in 1933 and last appearance was in 2010.)
2) A – Dwight Anderson (In 1979, he made 18 free throws in a victory over Mississippi State.)
3) D – 1946-47 (Kentucky finished the season 34-3.)
4) A – Yes (John Wall recorded 66 steals and Eric Bledsoe recorded 52.)
5) C – 9 (UK won every game played at Madison Square Garden from 1976-99.)
6) C – 38 (The Wildcats had winning seasons from 1927-28 to 1965-66.)
7) C – Kentucky State University (The name switched from Kentucky State College in 1908 and changed again to the University of Kentucky in 1917.)
8) A – Sky ("Blue, the sky that o'er us bends")
9) B – 34 (UK won every home opener from 1927-61 [UK did not play in 1952-53].)
10) A – 1940s (Three Wildcats were named Consensus First Team All-American a total of six times: Bob Brannum [1944], Ralph Beard [1947, 1948, 1949], Alex Groza [1947 and 1949].)
11) A – Wayne Turner (He had 238 career steals for the Wildcats from 1995-99.)
12) D – Jamal Mashburn (He scored 31 points versus Georgia in 1991.)
13) A – John Mauer (He coached Kentucky from 1928-30.)
14) A – Yes (John Wall was drafted No. 1 overall by the Washington Wizards in the 2010 NBA Draft.)

15) C – 34 points (This happened in both 1948 [UK 91,
    Louisville 57] and 1986 [UK 85, Louisville 51].)
16) B – 3 (Jon Hood [Madisonville, Ky.] Mark Krebs
    [Newport, Ky.], and Darius Miller [Maysville, Ky.])
17) A – Yes (The closest any coach with 500 or more wins
    comes to Rupp's .822 winning percentage is Roy
    Williams with a .798 winning percentage.)
18) D – Virginia Tech (The Wildcats fell 77-80 to the Hokies
    at home in 1962.)
19) D – Stainless page ("White, Kentucky's stainless page")
20) C – Managers (Managers ran the teams from 1903-09
    and combined for a 21-35 record, for a .375
    winning percentage. E.R. Sweetland became the
    first-ever paid basketball coach at UK for the 1910
    season.)
21) C – Tennessee (The Wildcats fell 65-74 to the
    Volunteers at Thompson-Boling Arena.)
22) B – No (Jamal Mashburn was never chosen as a team
    captain in his three years as a Wildcat.)
23) C – 51 (This is the most appearances of any school.)
24) A – 24 (In 1983 Kentucky and Cincinnati combined for a
    total of 35 points [UK 24, UC 11].)
25) B – 1951 (The first televised UK game was an NCAA
    Tournament game versus St. John's [UK 59, St.
    John's 43].)
26) C – 10 (1948, 1949, 1951, 1958, 1966, 1975, 1978,
    1996, 1997, and 1998)

27) B – 7 (Kentucky won the SEC Tournament Championship every year from 1944-50.)

28) A – Tom Payne (A 7'0" center from Louisville, he signed with Kentucky in 1969.)

29) C – 6 (In the 1988-89 season, the Wildcats finished sixth in the SEC with a conference record of 8-10. Kentucky had an overall record of 13-19 in Eddie Sutton's last season as head coach.)

30) A – Yes (The Wildcats went 247-24, for a .911 winning percentage. Rupp led his teams to a 203-8 record, for a .962 winning percentage during the last 20 years playing at Alumni Gym.)

31) D – Darius Miller (He made a three-pointer 41 seconds into the game against East Tennessee State to put UK in the lead 3-0.)

32) D – 86 (In 1996, UK scored 86 in the first half against LSU [UK 129, LSU 97].)

33) C – 23 (The last time UK lost while ranked No. 1 was to South Carolina on Jan. 26, 2010 [UK 62, USC 68].)

34) A – Three-pointers made (Kentucky led the nation in all other categories listed [3,325 total points scored, 776 assists, and 480 steals].)

35) B – 3 (Kentucky lost in SEC Tournament Championship game appearances in 1979, 1980, and 1982.)

36) B – 6 (H.J. Iddings, S.A. Boles, Andrew Gill, C.O. Applegran, Ray Eklund, and Basil Hayden)

37) C – 1997-98 (UK had 240 blocked shots in 39 games.)

38) A – Tennessee (The Wildcats fell 67-77 to the Volunteers in 1977.)

39) D – Tennessee (The Volunteers have a .316 winning percentage against the Wildcats.)

40) B – 7 (UK finished 8-7 at home in the 1966-67 season.)

41) C – 12 (Spanning 1945 to 1952)

42) A – Ralph Beard (He appeared on the cover in 1949, an edition published by Dell Publishing.)

43) D – Joe Hall (He held the first Midnight Practice at Kentucky in 1982.)

44) B – Rick Robey (He won a High School State Championship in 1974 with Brother Martin High School [New Orleans, LA], an NCAA Championship in 1978 with Kentucky, and an NBA Championship in 1981 with the Boston Celtics.)

45) C – 1921 (The Wildcats defeated Tulane, Mercer, Mississippi A&M, and Georgia to win the Southern Intercollegiate Athletic Association Conference Tournament. The SIAA was one of the nation's first collegiate athletic conferences. Every SEC team, except for Arkansas, was once a member.)

46) A – $3.00 (This money was used to buy the team basketball. Players were responsible for their own uniforms and shoes.)

47) D – 1996-97 (Kentucky averaged 83.1 points per game and only gave up 62.8 points per game. The Wildcats led the nation in scoring margin a total of eight seasons [1948-49, 1950-51, 1951-52, 1953-54, 1956-57, 1994-95, 1995-96, and 1996-97].)

48) B – 4 (C.M. Newton, Cliff Hagan, Frank Ramsey, and Dan Issel)

49) C – 4 (Kentucky came from behind following halftime to beat Miami [36-39 at half, 72-70 final], Stanford [32-38 at half, 73-65 final], Connecticut [23-29 at half, 64-61 final], and Georgia [34-35 at half, 76-68 final].)

50) C – 51 (Kentucky won every conference game from Jan. 28, 1950 until Jan. 8, 1955.)

Note: All answers valid as of the end of the 2009-10 season, unless otherwise indicated in the question itself.

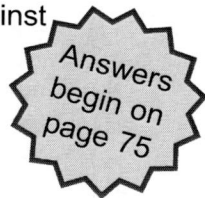

1) Does Kentucky have a winning record against every member of the Big Ten?

Answers begin on page 75

   A) Yes
   B) No

2) Which game set Kentucky's attendance record at Rupp Arena?

   A) Florida 2007
   B) Louisville 2005
   C) Louisville 2010
   D) LSU 1995

3) What is the highest AP ranked team an unranked Kentucky team has beaten?

   A) No. 1
   B) No. 4
   C) No. 6
   D) No. 7

4) What is UK's all-time lowest seed in the NCAA Tournament?

   A) No. 6
   B) No. 8
   C) No. 10
   D) No. 12

5) Who was Kentucky's first-ever SEC opponent?

A) Tulane
B) Tennessee
C) Alabama
D) Georgia Tech

6) What is UK's largest margin of victory over Tennessee?

A) 39 points
B) 46 points
C) 53 points
D) 61 points

7) Excluding Louisville, who is the last team from the state of Kentucky to beat the Wildcats?

A) Eastern Kentucky
B) Western Kentucky
C) Georgetown College
D) Union College

8) Who holds the Wildcat record for most points scored in a freshman year?

A) Sam Bowie
B) Jamal Mashburn
C) John Wall
D) Rex Chapman

9) Did Kentucky attempt more free throws than its opponents in the 2009-10 season?

    A) Yes
    B) No

10) What is UK's record for most rebounds as a team in a single game?

    A) 61
    B) 79
    C) 90
    D) 108

11) Which of the following UK players never scored 40 or more points in a single NCAA Tournament game?

    A) Tayshaun Prince
    B) Dan Issel
    C) Kenny Walker
    D) Jack Givens

12) Where was the first-ever Kentucky basketball game played?

    A) State College Gymnasium
    B) Buell Armory Gymnasium
    C) Wildcat Hall
    D) Romey Recreation Hall

13) In which category did Kentucky lead the nation in 1983?

    A)   Field-goal percentage
    B)   Fouls against
    C)   Free throws attempted
    D)   Technical fouls

14) When was the last time a No. 1-ranked Kentucky team lost to an unranked opponent?

    A)   1996
    B)   1998
    C)   2002
    D)   2010

15) How many times has Kentucky won 30 or more games in a season?

    A)   9
    B)   12
    C)   15
    D)   17

16) How many games did it take KU's Adolph Rupp to get to 500 career victories?

    A)   561
    B)   578
    C)   583
    D)   594

17) In the 2009-10 season, did any player for Kentucky have 10 or more turnovers in a single game?

    A) Yes
    B) No

18) How many total weeks has Kentucky held the top spot in the AP Poll?

    A) 62
    B) 75
    C) 81
    D) 91

19) When was the last season Kentucky scored over 3,000 points as a team?

    A) 1983-84
    B) 1992-93
    C) 1997-98
    D) 2009-10

20) What is Kentucky's record for most consecutive NCAA Tournament losses?

    A) 2
    B) 3
    C) 4
    D) 6

21) What is the combined winning percentage of Kentucky head coaches who lasted one season or less?

   A) .560
   B) .591
   C) .628
   D) .694

22) How many seasons has Kentucky led the nation in attendance?

   A) 16
   B) 17
   C) 22
   D) 25

23) Where did John Calipari coach before Kentucky?

   A) Illinois
   B) Villanova
   C) UMass
   D) Memphis

24) Which is the only ACC school with an all-time winning record against Kentucky?

   A) Boston College
   B) Duke
   C) Maryland
   D) North Carolina

25) When was UK's team record set for most points scored in a season?

    A) 1951-52
    B) 1977-78
    C) 1993-94
    D) 1996-97

26) Has Kentucky won 2,000 or more games?

    A) Yes
    B) No

27) How many times has Kentucky been a No. 1 seed in the NCAA Tournament?

    A) 5
    B) 8
    C) 10
    D) 13

28) Which one-season Kentucky head coach had the highest winning percentage?

    A) S.A. Boles
    B) Ray Eklund
    C) Andrew Gill
    D) Alpha Brumage

29) Which decade did UK have its lowest winning percentage?

    A) 1900s
    B) 1910s
    C) 1930s
    D) 1980s

30) What is Kentucky's record for most victories in a season?

    A) 30
    B) 32
    C) 36
    D) 37

31) How many Wildcats have scored 1,000 or more career points?

    A) 44
    B) 48
    C) 53
    D) 57

32) Against which major conference does Kentucky have the best record?

    A) Big East
    B) ACC
    C) Big Ten
    D) Big 12

33) What is UK's record for largest margin of victory in an NCAA Tournament game?

A) 35 points
B) 41 points
C) 46 points
D) 50 points

34) Which Wildcat had the highest three-point percentage in the 2009-10 season (min. 25 attempts)?

A) John Wall
B) Darnell Dodson
C) DeAndre Liggins
D) Eric Bledsoe

35) When was the most recent season the Wildcats made greater than 50 percent of their shots from the field?

A) 1985-86
B) 1994-95
C) 1997-98
D) 2002-03

36) Has Kentucky ever had five players drafted in the NBA Draft in the same year?

A) Yes
B) No

37) Who was the most recent player to lead Kentucky in scoring for three seasons?

    A) Jamal Mashburn
    B) Keith Bogans
    C) Tony Delk
    D) Kenny Walker

38) Each of Kentucky's National Championship teams also won the SEC regular season and conference tournament.

    A) True
    B) False

39) What is UK's record for most consecutive 30-win seasons?

    A) 2
    B) 3
    C) 5
    D) 6

40) How many times did UK players foul out of a game during the 2009-10 season?

    A) 5
    B) 7
    C) 10
    D) 13

41) How many Wildcats averaged greater than 20 minutes of playing time per game in the 2009-10 season?

A) 5
B) 6
C) 7
D) 9

42) Who was the most recent Wildcat to be named First Team Academic All-American?

A) Mark Pope
B) Bob Guyette
C) Chuck Verderber
D) Kyle Macy

43) Which of the following players did not score over 2,000 career points while at Kentucky?

A) Cotton Nash
B) Dan Issel
C) Jack Givens
D) Kenny Walker

44) What is UK's longest losing streak in Rupp Arena?

A) 1 game
B) 2 games
C) 4 games
D) 5 games

45) Who is the only Kentucky player to be awarded SEC Defensive Player of the Year?

A) Chuck Hayes
B) Sam Bowie
C) Melvin Turpin
D) Jamaal Magloire

46) Where did John Calipari play college basketball?

A) Butler
B) Sam Houston State
C) Youngstown State
D) Clarion

47) Does Kentucky have a losing record against any of the five major conferences (Big Ten, Big 12, Pac-10, ACC, or Big East)?

A) Yes
B) No

48) Which school has beaten Kentucky more than once in Freedom Hall?

A) Georgia
B) Ohio State
C) Notre Dame
D) Vanderbilt

49) What team did the USA Olympic team, led by five Kentucky players, beat to win the gold medal in 1948?

A) Spain
B) China
C) Russia
D) France

50) Which team broke Kentucky's 129-game home court winning streak?

A) Georgia Tech
B) Vanderbilt
C) Tennessee
D) Notre Dame

Kentucky hired E.R. Sweetland as its new football coach in 1909. Sweetland immediately led UK to a record of 9-1, outscoring opponents 261-29. Kentucky hoped his winning way on the gridiron would lead to wins on the hard court too. The school had been considering cancelling its basketball program, but instead hired Sweetland as UK's head basketball coach for the 1910 season. Illness caused Sweetland to miss various games and the team finished 4-8 his first season. In 1912, his only other season as UK head coach, Sweetland led the Wildcats to a record of 9-0, its first-ever undefeated season. In football, Sweetland led the Wildcats to a 23-5 (.821) record in three seasons. Mired in controversy regarding the use of ineligible athletes and arson accusations, Sweetland resigned from his coaching duties in 1913.

1) A – Yes (UK has a winning record against every Big Ten member and holds an all-time record of 94-56 vs. the conference, for a .627 winning percentage.)

2) C – Louisville 2010 (On Jan. 2, 2010, 24,479 Wildcat fans packed Rupp Arena to see UK beat the Cardinals 71-62.)

3) B – No. 4 (In 2001, unranked Kentucky beat No. 4 Tennessee 84-74 and in 1961 the unranked Wildcats beat No. 4 Kansas State 80-67.)

4) D – No. 12 (The Wildcats made it to the Sweet 16 in 1985 before losing to No. 1 seed St John's, 70-86.)

5) A – Tulane (The SEC was formed in 1932 and Tulane was a member until 1966.)

6) D – 61 points (In 1993, UK beat the Volunteers 101-40.)

7) B – Western Kentucky (In 1971, Kentucky lost 83-107 to the Hilltoppers.)

8) C – John Wall (Wall totaled 616 points scored in 37 games in 2009-10 for a 16.6 average.)

9) A – Yes (The Wildcats attempted 971 free throws while their opponents attempted 688.)

10) D – 108 (UK set this record against Ole Miss in 1964.)

11) C – Kenny Walker (His highest total was 32 points [Dan Issel 44 points, Jack Givens 41, and Tayshaun Prince 41].)

12) A – State College Gymnasium (This was renamed Buell Armory in 1910.)

13) A – Field-goal percentage (As a team, UK was 869-1,564 from the floor, for a .556 percentage made.)

14) D – 2010 (The last time UK lost to an unranked opponent while ranked No. 1 was to South Carolina on Jan. 26, 2010 [UK 62, USC 68]. Kentucky has lost a total of thirteen times to unranked opponents while holding the top spot in the AP Poll.)

15) B – 12 (1947, 1948, 1949, 1951, 1978, 1986, 1993, 1996, 1997, 1998, 2003, and 2010)

16) C – 583 (Rupp is the fastest, in NCAA coaching history, to achieve 500 victories.)

17) B – No (The most turnovers by a player were seven by John Wall [four times] & Eric Bledsoe [two times].)

18) C – 81 (The last time the Wildcats held the No. 1 spot in the AP Poll was in the 11th week of 2009-10.)

19) D – 2009-10 (The Wildcats scored a total of 3,012 points for an average of 79.3 points per game.)

20) B – 3 (This has happened three different times: 1962-1964, 1970-1971, and 1980-1982 [1964 and 1971 includes losses in consolation games].)

21) A – .560 (One-season or less UK head coaches have a combined record of 51-40-1.)

22) C – 22 (UK led the NCAA in attendance from 1977-84, 1996-04, and 2006-10. The attendance average in 2009-10 was 24,110, a Rupp Arena record.)

23) D – Memphis (Calipari coached the Tigers to a record of 252-69 [.785] from the 2000-01 season through the 2008-09 season.)

24) D – North Carolina (UK has an all-time record of 11-21 vs. the Tar Heels, for a .344 winning percentage.)

25) D – 1996-97 (The Wildcats scored 3,325 points in 40 games, for an average of 83.1 points per game.)

26) A – Yes (Kentucky has an overall record of 2,024-638-1, for a .760 winning percentage.)

27) C – 10 (1980, 1984, 1986, 1993, 1995, 1996, 1997, 2003, 2004, and 2010. Seeding in the tournament did not begin until 1979.)

28) B – Ray Eklund (He had a .833 winning percentage with a record of 15-3 in 1926.)

29) A – 1900s (UK went 25-43 [.368 winning percentage].)

30) C – 36 (In 1947-48, the Wildcats finished 36-3.)

31) D – 57 (Jodie Meeks and Patrick Patterson joined the 1,000 career points club following the 2008-09 season. Patterson added to his career point total in 2009-10 and ranks 13th all-time with 1,564 points. Meeks is ranked 34th with 1,246 points.)

32) D – Big 12 (The Wildcats are 54-9, for a winning percentage of .857 against Big 12 teams.)

33) C – 46 points (UK beat St. Mary's 113-67 in 1995.)

34) D – Eric Bledsoe (He shot 49-128 from three-point range, for .383 percent.)

35) A – 1985-86 (Kentucky made 1,030 of 2,003 attempts, for a percentage of 51.4. The NCAA introduced the three-point line the following season.)

36) A – Yes (UK had five players drafted in the 2010 NBA Draft [John Wall, DeMarcus Cousins, Patrick Patterson, Eric Bledsoe, and Daniel Orton]. UK had four players drafted in the same year six times: 1949, 1975, 1978, 1984, 1988, and 1996.)

37) C – Tony Delk (He led the Wildcats in scoring from 1994-96. The only other players to lead the team in scoring for three years are Jack Givens and Cotton Nash.)

38) B – False (All but one of Kentucky's NCAA Championship teams finished first in the SEC regular season and won the conference tournament. The 1996 National Championship team won the SEC regular season but lost 73-84 to Mississippi State in the SEC Tournament Championship game.)

39) B – 3 (This has happened two different times: 1947-49 and again from 1996-98.)

40) D – 13 (John Wall [1], DeAndre Liggins [1], Patrick Patterson [1], Eric Bledsoe [1], Darius Miller [2], DeMarcus Cousins [2], and Daniel Orton [5])

41) A – 5 (John Wall [34.8], Patrick Patterson [33.0], Eric Bledsoe [30.3], DeMarcus Cousins [23.5], and Darius Miller [21.2])

42) D – Kyle Macy (He was named First Team Academic All-American in 1979.)

43) A – Cotton Nash (He scored 1,770 career points [Dan Issel 2,138 points, Kenny Walker 2,080 points, and Jack Givens 2,038 points].)

44) B – 2 games (The Wildcats have never lost three or more in a row at Rupp Arena and have only lost two in a row on five occasions.)

45) A – Chuck Hayes (He was named SEC Defensive Player of the Year by the coaches in 2005.)

46) D – Clarion (After beginning his playing career at UNC Wilmington, Calipari transferred to Clarion to play point guard for the Eagles as a junior and senior.)

47) B – No (UK's records [including winning percentage] against the major conferences are: Big Ten 94-56 [.627], ACC 122-61 [.677], Pac-10 22-10 [.688], Big East 165-69 [.705], and Big 12 54-9 [.857].)

48) C – Notre Dame (Kentucky leads the series against the Fighting Irish at Freedom Hall 18-4, for a .818 winning percentage.)

49) D – France (The team included five Wildcats: Cliff Barker, Ralph Beard, Alex Groza, Wallace Jones, and Kenny Rollins. USA beat France 65-21.)

50) A – Georgia Tech (The Wildcats fell 58-59 to the Yellow Jackets on Jan. 8, 1955. This particular streak started against Ft. Knox on Jan. 4, 1943.)

Note: All answers valid as of the end of the 2009-10 season, unless otherwise indicated in the question itself.

1) Where did Adolph Rupp coach before Kentucky?

Answers begin on page 83

   A) Kansas
   B) Milan (Ind.) High School
   C) Tennessee
   D) Freeport (Ill.) High School

2) How many times has Kentucky begun the season ranked No. 1 in the first AP Poll?

   A) 2
   B) 3
   C) 4
   D) 6

3) Kentucky is undefeated against how many conferences (all current members of the conference)?

   A) 8
   B) 10
   C) 12
   D) 14

4) Did Billy Gillispie win his first-ever SEC conference game as head coach of Kentucky?

   A) Yes
   B) No

5) When was the first season a player at Kentucky averaged double figures for scoring?

A) 1915-16
B) 1920-21
C) 1924-25
D) 1929-30

6) What was Kentucky's nickname prior to Wildcats?

A) Mountaineers
B) Rebels
C) Musketeers
D) Cadets

7) Which player holds Kentucky's record for most points scored in an NCAA Championship game?

A) Jack Givens
B) Scott Padgett
C) Tony Delk
D) Vernon Hatton

8) How many Kentucky players have been drafted in the first round of the NBA Draft?

A) 12
B) 17
C) 21
D) 26

9) What were Kentucky's original chosen colors?

    A) Black and Gold
    B) Green and White
    C) Gray and Orange
    D) Blue and Light Yellow

10) How many times did Kentucky trail at halftime in an NCAA Championship game they went on to win?

    A) 0
    B) 3
    C) 4
    D) 6

Wildcatology Trivia Challenge

1) D – Freeport (Ill.) High School
2) C – 4 (1950-51, 1951-52, 1980-81, and 1995-96)
3) B – 10 (America East 5-0, Big Sky 2-0, Colonial 5-0,
     Metro Atlantic 12-0, Mid Eastern 4-0, Ohio Valley
     33-0, Southern 19-0, Southwestern 4-0, and
     Western Athletic 7-0 for a combined 91-0.)
4) A – Yes (UK beat Georgia 76-68 to give Calipari a win in
     his first-ever conference game on Jan. 9, 2010.)
5) A – 1915-16 (Derrill Hart averaged 13.3 points per
     game.)
6) D – Cadets (UK athletes were known as the Cadets until
     1909 when they became known as the Wildcats.)
7) A – Jack Givens (He scored 41 points in the 1978 NCAA
     Championship game against Duke.)
8) D – 26 (The five players selected in the 2010 NBA Draft
     were the most recent to join the list.)
9) D – Blue and Light Yellow (Students decided on these
     colors in 1891 before dropping those colors for the
     official Blue and White.)
10) B – 3 (1951, 1958, and 1998)

Note: All answers valid as of the end of the 2009-10
season, unless otherwise indicated in the question
itself.

Player / Team Score Sheet

Name:_____

Preseason			Regular Season			Conference Tournament			Championship Game			Overtime Bonus	
1	26		1	26		1	26		1	26		1	
2	27		2	27		2	27		2	27		2	
3	28		3	28		3	28		3	28		3	
4	29		4	29		4	29		4	29		4	
5	30		5	30		5	30		5	30		5	
6	31		6	31		6	31		6	31		6	
7	32		7	32		7	32		7	32		7	
8	33		8	33		8	33		8	33		8	
9	34		9	34		9	34		9	34		9	
10	35		10	35		10	35		10	35		10	
11	36		11	36		11	36		11	36			
12	37		12	37		12	37		12	37			
13	38		13	38		13	38		13	38			
14	39		14	39		14	39		14	39			
15	40		15	40		15	40		15	40			
16	41		16	41		16	41		16	41			
17	42		17	42		17	42		17	42			
18	43		18	43		18	43		18	43			
19	44		19	44		19	44		19	44			
20	45		20	45		20	45		20	45			
21	46		21	46		21	46		21	46			
22	47		22	47		22	47		22	47			
23	48		23	48		23	48		23	48			
24	49		24	49		24	49		24	49			
25	50		25	50		25	50		25	50			
___ x 1 =___			___ x 2 =___			___ x 3 =___			___ x 4 =___			___ x 4 =___	

Multiply total number correct by point value/quarter to calculate totals for each quarter.

Add total of all quarters below.

Total Points:_____

Thank you for playing *Wildcatology Trivia Challenge*.

Additional score sheets are available at:
www.TriviaGameBooks.com